MISSIO DEI

IN THE CRISIS OF CHRISTIANITY

FRED PEATROSS

Published in the United States by Cold Tree Press
Nashville, Tennessee
www.coldtreepress.com

© 2007 Fred Peatross. All rights reserved.
Cover Design © 2007 Cold Tree Press
All photographs and graphics by Fred Peatross

This book may not be reproduced in any form without express written permission.

Printed in the United States of America
ISBN 978-1-58385-185-2

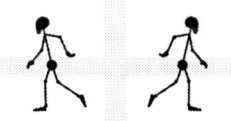

PRAISE FOR MISSIO DEI:
IN THE CRISIS OF CHRISTIANITY

The divine surprises us in the mundane. In Ordinary Time, in the liminal, half-light of life - it is in the lived, imperfect moments where God works the most mystery in our souls. Which is exactly why Fred Peatross' loving little piece is so needed now. Can the Church turn from presenting God to being present with God and with the world God loves - yes, in all its ordinariness? That is the question.

—Sally Morgenthaler;
Author and innovator in Christian practices

In a cultural environment increasingly cynical about Christianity in general and consumer church in particular, Fred Peatross invites us to 'come and see' a Christ who has left the (church) building to lovingly touch the world – one conversation at a time - on this journey we humans call life. Rather than evangelism being a 'program' of the church, sharing the Gospel becomes a way of being in the world. This is good news indeed!

—John York; Preaching Minister,
Family of God at Woodmont Hills;
Professor of Bible and Preaching, Lipscomb University

Fred Peatross has earned the highest compliment a non-Christian can bestow on a follower of Jesus. They call Fred a 'different kind of Christian'

—Jim Henderson;
Author of *a.k.a. Lost*
Off the Map <http://www.off-the-map.org/>

The world is in disruption; personally, locally, throughout humanity. It's a fact and we all feel it. Fred helps us get our balance and reconnect the many fragmenting dots by giving us examples of where we can find firm footing. In a fluid world Fred points out that our relationship with Christ is more than an event – it is a relationship. He helps us put the horse back in front of the cart and rediscover our call to a post-post modern world.

—Rex Miller;
Author/Futurist *The Millennium Matrix: Reclaiming the Past and Reframing the Future of the Church*
www.millenniummatrix.com

We now live with so many choices that the temptation is to live only in the moment. Yet spirituality, like missionality, requires attention and intention. Fred calls us to live missionally and intentionally.
—Len Hjalmarson; author, Kelowna, British Columbia

The Church is in need of something much deeper than new methods for evangelism. We are in need of a map to get us back to a more authentic path of discipling people into the kingdom. Fred Peatross gives us an important piece of that map here.

—Will Samson; coordinator for Emergent Village

Perhaps you're burned out on church because you thought "being involved" and "plugged in" was the secret to church happiness. Read this book if you want to know how a "different kind of Christian" thinks and acts. Most important will be the knowledge that you can become a missionary right where you.
—**Greg Taylor; Managing Editor:** *New Wineskins Magazine* **ministering with the Garnett Church in Tulsa**

Like the legendary Rip Van Winkle, many of us are waking up to realize that the world is far different than we last remember it. With that realization also comes the awareness that we scarcely know how to talk to the people who inhabit this new world. God has graciously given us sisters and brothers like Fred Peatross to observe, analyze and help us form relationships in which to communicate the ancient gospel to our contemporary comrades.
– **Edward Fudge; Author of** *The Fire that Consumes* **and** *Beyond the Sacred Pages*

"One size fits all" has always been a myth regardless of whether it referred to underwear, worship, or evangelism. Fred helps us break out of the sacred bubble of Sunday morning and move Christianity into its rightful place – the real world.
—**Patrick Meade; Preaching Minister and Professor; Rochester Hills, Michigan**

It is said that true evangelism is simply one hungry man informing another hungry man where to find bread. Fred Peatross is a hungry man who has found Bread, and simply seeks to share that source of life with others. He has called us to move from methods to missions; from programs to people. As we journey to our eternal destination, he has simply challenged us to issue the same invitation to others as Moses extended to Hobab: "Come with us, and we will do you good." You will be refreshed by his insights, and strengthened for the journey ahead.

—Al Maxey; Minister/Elder:
Alamogordo, New Mexico
Author of *"Down, But Not Out"*
and a weekly series known as "Reflections"

In this excellent book Fred Peatross encourages us to follow the "Guide" as He transforms every institutional program in moving from the attractional mode to missional.

—Jeff Garrett
Norway Avenue Church
Huntington, WV

TABLE OF CONTENTS

Preface	xiii
Foreword by Michael Frost	xv
Introduction	xviit
PART ONE DECONSTRUCTION	1
The Attractional Church Mode and the Missional Church Mode	3
The Forging of New Gospel Communities	13
PART TWO RECONSTRUCTION	27
Evolution of an Emerging	29
A Missional Mechanism for the Attractional Church	43
Think Globally Act Neighborly	61
The Importance of Perception	71
Determined	79
Epilogue	83
Appendix	89

MISSIO DEI

IN THE CRISIS OF CHRISTIANITY

PREFACE
BY FRED PEATROSS

The church has a limited perception on infinite reality. And with a grandiloquent self-assurance, it imposes that perception on its members until they think it's their own. For decades, the church has wrapped itself in a cocoon of realities professed by the generations who came before us. It is a cocoon that gives God's people a sense of security through the shared connections of a common understanding of the way the church ministers.

Incongruous as it may be, I have always both accepted and rejected the church's view of what is appropriate. I admit I hunger for the comfort that can come from devotion to herd wisdom. At the same time, I remain desperate to flee the soul-wilting cover of "doing ministry as always" to fly the more uncertain course of connecting with those Jesus is seeking through unconventional, innovative, and fresh ways.

HOW TO BE OF OPTIMUM VALUE IN AN ATTRACTIONAL CHURCH
(while staying out of the cocoon)

Okay, I'll say it. I'm a renegade and, by definition, renegades resist being led. They oppose policy, procedure, conformity, compliance, rigidity, and submission to status quo while living tangentially in originality, rule breaking, non-conformity, experimentation, and innovation. Renegades fly a course related to the system but not of the system. This inimitable path orbits outside the gravitational pull of the church but close enough to keep from spinning out into deep space.

To be of optimal value in an attractional church, I invest enough individuality to counteract the pull of *church gravity* but not so much that I escape the pull altogether - just enough to stay out of the cocoon.

It's unfortunate that the church has confused the expression of a lifestyle with its purpose.

FORWARD

The term "emerging" has become so loaded by the hopes and fears of various sectors of the church community that it's hard to use it without offending some, exciting others, and raising the suspicions of yet others. Fred Peatross offers us a very useful introduction to the seismic shifts that are occurring within the Western church, and by so doing, he helps to dispel the hysteria and anxieties many Christians feel toward anything emergent.

Fred rightly points out that various forces within the church are aligning and cross-pollinating and developing a new and potentially exciting approach to following Christ in the 21st Century. Whether it be the urban mission sector or the post-evangelicals, whether the radical discipleship movement or the Gospel and Our Culture guys inspired as they were by Lesslie Newbigin and David Bosch[1], whether it be the house church movement or the alternative worship crowd or the new monastics or the new evangelicals, it seems that their

---

[1] Christian theologians involved in missiology and the Gospel & Our Culture Movement.

thinking is being cross-fertilized and their energy for mission is being aligned in a way that augurs well for the future of the Western church.

With so many different movements coming slowly together, we need thinkers like Fred Peatross to make this complex, new movement understandable and accessible.

Read this book and then read it again. It will introduce you to the coming brave new world of Christian mission.

—Michael Frost
Morling College, Sydney
author of *Exiles and The Shaping of Things to Come*

INTRODUCTION

We sat together and drank our latte as we engaged in conversation. Knowing each other for almost 20 years enabled us to transparently move from the latest news on the home front to the state of our spiritual walks to the desires and dreams of our futures. That exchange cleared the way for the primary reason for our meeting at Starbucks on this particular day: to discuss the analysis in my writings about a phrase used on the footer of a church bulletin: "Creating environments that connect us with Jesus and people."

I take the position that the Christian community no longer lives in a favored position with its host culture[2] and to reach this culture, Christians must be more like leaven than a church-centric, attractional-Sunday-center. Individually, many of us are in missional-praxis, but if the established, conventional church is to survive the next decade, its leaders must start thinking with a corporate responsibility and accountability laudable in building a culture of Christians who strategically

---

[2] An un-favored position with the host culture is evidenced by the numerous court cases challenging everything from the Pledge of Allegiance's 'one nation under God,' to prayer in public school. Over the last decade cohabitation has exceeded commitment through the vows of marriage. Christianity no longer has a strong moral voice in western society.

"go" to the missing in their environment. But as Neil Cole says, "you have to be willing to sit in the smoking section when your primary stance is missional."

I find a degree of difficulty in articulating a primary missional stance. Reflecting on the conversation that day, I must concede that my failure to expressively characterize the differences between the attractional mode and the missional mode shortsighted my friend, which limited the capacity of his scope, breadth, and range. Because I failed to rework his church lens environment, he mistakenly walked away believing we agreed in principle. I walked away confused by the conversation.

As a seasoned church minister with over 20 years' experience, my friend understood missional as anyone with a resume like his would—through the prism of the institutional church. Whether attractional, seeker, or traditional, the primary lens any church employee sees ministry through is what I refer to as the "church myopia lens."[3]

At times, my friend broke through the institutional

---

[3] Cecil Hook tells the following story.

"After ten years with this church, I resigned my preaching commitment and took a janitorial job with the same church. This was necessary for supplementing my Social Security income. That enabled me to retire. After several years of retirement, when my wife was able to draw Social Security benefits, we terminated the janitorial contract.

When we received our last paycheck from the church, even for janitorial work, we felt a freedom, which we had never experienced before. We came to realize more than ever before that we had spent our career in helping to build and entrench an oppressive system of organized, sectarian religion. That system overpowers the life and conscience of the devotee and stifles the freedom of individual initiative in using the God-given talent." –Cecil Hook; Free to Change, chapter 1

church curtain to characterize a personal ministry that extended beyond the church campus. There was no reason to dispute this. I already knew he cared about people and their place in salvation's process. Our differences in understanding are at the corporate level.

It's important to mention that I'm not totally, 100-percent opposed to the attractional mode.[4] What I am opposed to is

---

[4]An approach to Christian mission in which the church develops programs, meetings, services, or other "products" in order to attract unbelievers into the influences of the Christian community. While there is an element to which the New Testament church was attractive and enjoyed the favor of the broader community (in some contexts), the contemporary church has come to a place where it almost totally relies on an attractional approach to its community. -from the glossary of The Shaping of Things to Come -Alan Hirsch

church leadership taking the primary stance that by tweaking, or making relevant, the weekly "church worship service" the people Jesus misses will come, stand in line, and like a Saturday night rock concert rush the entrance once the door is opened. A "come-to-church" priority has unknowingly and insipidly taken precedence over "come-to-Jesus." And "come-to-church" disturbs those of a missional persuasion.

Will you do me a favor? Get yourself some coffee, a latte, or mocha and give me an hour of your time. Let's listen to the rhythms of culture and Scripture. Let's listen to the voices. Let's consider the transitions. And most of all, let's observe the one they call the Savior. And let's see if we can find the varied elements that matter in this third millennium.

DECONSTRUCTION

THE ATTRACTIONAL CHURCH MODE
AND THE MISSIONAL CHURCH MODE

A Metaphorical Narrative:
The Attractional Church

The hands were raised high. The applause from the thousands of troops crowded into the Center for the United Service Organization[5] show was loud and enthusiastic.

The Air Force General, the chairman of the Joint Chiefs of Staff, and four USO celebrities were there as part of an entertainment tour that began the previous Sunday in Germany.

The Air Force General took the stage, prior to the start of the USO show to re-enlist 45 service members. The members all walked forward and stood before the podium.

Following the re-enlistment, the Joint Chief of Staff told the troops he was happy to be in "hoorah country," adding, "I have heard General Minister have conversations where all he says to his secretary is 'hoorah.'"

The General thanked the troops for their service and told them to look around to see who wasn't there and to go back

---

[5]"The USO is a private, nonprofit organization whose mission is to provide morale, welfare, and recreation-type services to the men and women in uniform. The original intent of Congress — and enduring style of USO delivery — is to represent the American people by extending a touch of home to the military." From the home page of uso.org

and invite them to come.

After the Joint Chief of Staff and the General left the stage, the singers took their places and began the evening with a song all were familiar with. The soldiers joined in as they sang into the evening.

The Embedded Nature Of The Attractional Paradigm: Two Examples

"It would be cool to write your own variety-type show and have some live musical pieces interspersed throughout the performance dedicating music to certain events and people in or related to the congregation. Then have some comedy routines using actual events from the congregation. Throughout the show you could use black-and-white video clips of what it means to be an American. Then you could end the performance with a video clip or slide show with pictures and events from WWII."[6]

"This Sunday is Easter. It is a great time to invite your family and friends to church. Many people are receptive to invitations during the holidays but you have to ask them. It's easy to ask a friend to church. All you need to say is, "Please come to church with me this Easter.""[7]

---

[6]From the Church Media Network Forum <http://www.churchmedia.net/CMN/drama-and-music/6957-uso-type-show-ideas.html>
[7]Taken from a church bulletin

A Metaphorical Narrative: The Missional Church

While the United States Military is busy stabilizing Afghanistan and Iraq, the leaders in the American military are busy plotting new strategy. The primary stance of this strategy is missional.

Men and women of the military are being sent to different parts of the world to establish "peace communities." One such place is the Horn of Africa where troops are digging wells, training the native population in construction trades, and providing health care to both the people and their livestock. Mission first: win the hearts of the people and eliminate the potential for terrorist safe havens. On the back end of the mission: training of indigenous tribes to fight the terrorists. If a terrorist challenge extends the tribes beyond their abilities, the Americans provide military support.

> Members of a relatively small U.S. military force based in the Horn of Africa have been called "aid workers with guns." The American troops are drilling wells,

> vaccinating livestock, building school facilities and performing a variety of other humanitarian missions in Djibouti. They have weapons, but their mission is to defeat terrorism without using force. Local people in the mostly Muslim region welcome the assistance.
>
> —Malcolm Brown

The future posture of the established, attractional church will not be known any time soon. The question on the radar screen of many is will she continue to operate as a USO-style delivery system relying upon professionalism to engage the assembly with homilies and praise songs while encouraging members to invite their neighbors, co-workers, and friends? Will that continue to be her primary stance? Or will she awaken to the reality of her un-favored position with her host culture and adopt a missionary stance as the American military has with its newly adopted strategy?

> Churches can lose their way -lose their sense of identity, their focus, the purpose and mission for which Christ has called them into their local community and into the world. When that happens, there is a real need for new and intensive "turnaround" strategies so that once more the flame may burn brightly, in what is otherwise often a very dark world.
> —Dr. George Bullard, Jr.

The Times Demand A Missional Stance

In the last half of the book of Luke and throughout the book of Acts, the reader encounters a series of road stories. Everyone is going somewhere. You find Jesus on the Emmaus road, Phillip on the road to Gaza, Peter on the road to Cornelius, Paul on the road to Damascus. If you're the least bit curious you have to ask, "Where is everyone going?" And the answer is they are moving away from their spiritual center—Jerusalem—and out into the world. As one reads the New Testament, especially the book of Acts, it becomes apparent that Christianity is depicted as a movement away from the center of religious activity and out into the fringes of the mission field looking for those Jesus misses the most.

Jesus' portability was seen in the inordinate amount of time he spent with prostitutes, tax collectors, government officials, and fishermen. Our addiction to centripetal ministry has kept us away from those Jesus misses. We've been called to leave our Temple and enter the court of the Gentiles to engage the "missing" on their territory[8] - territory comfortable and familiar to them, where government officials assemble for city council meetings, where art museum curators show their prizes, and where the missing ones willingly sit with "people of the way" to discuss life issues over a glass of wine or a latte. Reaching this emerging generation requires Christians to step out of the boat of church life and into the streams of culture in pursuit of something unprecedented, even downright miraculous. It means we replace our preoccupation with church and begin to walk the fringes of the mission field looking for those Jesus misses.

---

[8] The Court of the Gentiles was the one place on temple grounds where Jews and Gentiles could mingle together.

Church Then And Church Now

The church of the first century was a marginalized, subversive, persecuted, movement. But when Constantine came to the throne of the Roman Empire and granted Christians the freedom to assemble, everything changed. The Roman Emperor had gone from principle persecutor to chief sponsor of the church. In virtually an instant, the Christian Church found itself in a favored position with its host culture. With

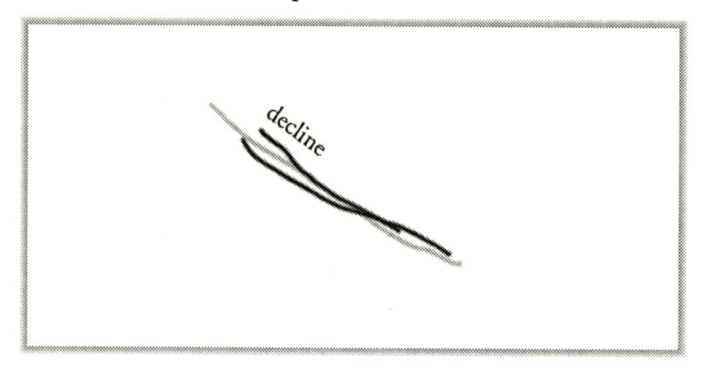

decline

this new church-state partnership Christians no longer needed to gather secretly in the homes of its members. Through the centuries, the church's favored position changed the social and religious patterns of Europe. She was the voice and pillar of the European culture and the metanarrative[9] for an entire age.

But for the last 250 years, Christianity has been in decline.

---

[9] An overarching story claiming to contain truth for all people for all times in culture.

Historians have referred to this period as the post-Christian era. Christianity no longer defines the broader culture. Once again, Christianity finds itself in an un-favored position with its host culture. This is evidenced by the frequency of divorce, the acceptance of cohabitation, the court cases challenging the Ten Commandments and the Pledge of Allegiance's "one nation under God." Yet the attractional church continues to do ministry in the context of a favored position with its host culture when in reality she is in a post-Enlightenment, post-Christian era.

> We must find the courage to leave our temples and enter the suffering-filled temples of human experience.
>
> —Preah Maha Ghosananda, the Gandhi of Cambodia

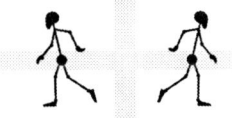

THE FORGING OF
NEW GOSPEL COMMUNITIES

Some believe churches that focused on growth in numbers have evangelism as their mission. While this may be true for some churches subscribing to church-growth philosophy and practice, there are some aspects of church growth that run contrary to missional church philosophies and practices.

First, missional churches focus on kingdom growth rather than church growth. Second, missional churches are more likely to focus on birthing new gospel communities rather than attempting to resurrect established churches that do not and cannot exhibit the characteristics of a movement simply because they are on the downside of the organizational curve.

> When one stops to consider the differences between the traditional and missional churches,

> we are faced with a stark dissimilarity between the two. If a traditional church wants to become missional, a radical transformation is necessary because the traditional church is a near-polar opposite of missional church!
>
> —Webb Kline

If it is not yet obvious, the greatest task for those of a missional persuasion will be calling the attractional church to its primary task—mission to a post-Christian society.[10] If mission becomes their priority, attractional churches will face a striking paradigm change. A renewed commitment to the missional task will require creativity in developing new forms and shapes in which the gospel can be expressed in a post-Christian culture.

---

[10] Post-Christian is a term used to describe a personal world view, religious movement or society that is no longer rooted in the language and assumptions of Christianity, though it had previously been in an environment of ubiquitous Christianity (Christendom). A post-Christian world then is one where Christianity is no longer the dominant civil religion, but one that has changed to embrace values, culture, and worldviews that are not necessarily Christian. – Wikipedia Encyclopedia

Imagine it's your goal to build a perfectly square building in the perfect center of a perfectly square piece of property. After much ado (with lots of tears and blood and sweat and laughter) you succeed. And you celebrate. You invite others to join you in your perfectly square building that's built in the perfect center of your perfectly square piece of property. And then a surveyor shows up. He informs you that what you thought were the boundaries of your property line is not, in fact, accurate. You are off center by about a foot-and-a-half.

What do you do? Maybe if you got everyone in the building to come and push. Or maybe you could get some to pull and some to push. Maybe you could even get some to pull, some to push and some to march around then pray. At some point in time, someone's going to get the idea that to meet your stated objective, you've either got to tear the whole thing down and start again—or go find another piece of property and let someone else live in the off-center building. Once the foundation's laid, it is where it is.

—John Alan Turner

In the end, many Christ-followers may have to walk away from the established church for the birthing of new gospel communities. If this becomes the reality, it is crucial that these new communities do not rely upon the redistribution of existing church members but engage those whom Jesus misses the most. Church leaders must ask questions about strategy, listen carefully within post-Christian culture, and develop queries in which the gospel can provide answers. Listening means our primary relationships are with those on the other side of Christianity. Effective strategy will depend on this.

It's important to note that listening to culture does not mean we reduce[11] the gospel. It simply recognizes that the New Testament has the resources to help the Christ-follower connect with the host culture. Like Jesus in His time, we incarnate culture and join the indigenous practices of our day – communally as well as individually. Patiently, we first do mission and allow the progression to naturally flow into indigenous gospel communities.[12]

> The "church" situation reminds me of when we started home schooling. We had to detoxify from

---

[11] To bring to a weaker state or condition.
[12] Alan Hirsch posits that incarnational mission engages people from within their cultural expression. Only in this way can the church actually become part of the cultural fabric and social rhythms of the host community.

public schools. The temptation was to bring in school desks and a blackboard and have "public school" in our house—to fall back on what we grew up with and were comfortable with. But that's not home schooling. Home schooling requires a change of mindset. Now, schooling takes place when we get up and go to bed, when we're watching TV, driving in a car, or going to a play. Of course, it also takes place in more structured lessons (book learning) as well. I said all that to say this… I thought I was pretty comfortable with non-conventional church. I'm finding

> that I need to detoxify. At times I'm tempted to plant a traditional Christian Church franchise but almost immediately something inside me curls up in the fetal position and starts rocking back and forth. "Traditional" is not where the Lord is taking us.
>
> —Jessie Perry, church planter

Birthing new gospel communities is not about cloning modern churches. Why reproduce something in decline? Fresh and new communities are able to build from the foundation up. In summary the challenge is twofold:

- *To creatively engage culture*[13] and
- *through influence, help existing attractional churches*

---

[13] There are many ways Christians could engage culture. One example would be to commission two or three college age Christ-followers to incarnate a paticular culture by renting a couple of apartments adjacent to each other and in close proximity to a local bar. These Christians would gather in the bar several times a week and sit with and get to know members of the local community. The bar becomes a gospel community. Alan Hirsch and Michael Frost refer to these venues as "third-places." The suggestion is the church is the "first-place." A person's residence is second place, but a bar, club, coffee house, etc is a "third-place" community.

> *transform into missional communities that contextualizes the gospel in a post-enlightenment era.*[14]

The most valuable lesson I learned as a shepherd in an attractional church was when you're of the emergent/missional persuasion, you stop exerting your energy and time with a group of leaders set in their orbit. Exchange your time and energy for the birthing of new communities. This frees the creative leader to pioneer a movement as opposed to always attempting to lead from the downside of an organization's growth curve.

> We are still too event oriented, a model passed down to us from another time. For most people today receiving Christ will happen at the end of a process and that takes time. Outreach events have their place but are no longer the "end all" of our evangelistic

---

[14] A European intellectual movement of the 17th and 18th centuries in which ideas concerning God, reason, nature, and man were synthesized into a worldview that gained wide assent and that instigated revolutionary developments in art, philosophy, and politics. Central to Enlightenment thought were the use and the celebration of reason, the power by which man understands. –Encyclopedia Britannica

> activity as they may have been in the former paradigm. The beginning of the process is all about building relationships. Our challenge is in culture-building—to help church members develop trusting and meaningful relationships with the people Jesus misses the most.

Theological Differences Between The Established Church And The Missional Church

The theological difference between the established church and the missional church begins with how one understands church. Theologians call this ecclesiology.[15] A missional ecclesiology is rooted in God's character and purpose as a sending God. God sent his Son, the Son sends the Spirit, and the Spirit sends the Church.[16] As Jesus was the fullness of God incarnate, the missional church follows Jesus' model and continues the

---

[15] The branch of theology that is concerned with the nature, constitution, and functions of a church

[16] Matthew 28:18-20; John 20:21; Acts 1:8

presence of Jesus in the world—participating as the second incarnation—an extension of God's presence in the world. In summary:

- *Missional churches are deeply connected to the community. The church is not focused on its facility but is focused on living and representing the One he follows as he walks alongside the people Jesus misses*
- *Missional churches are indigenous. They have taken root in the soil and reflect, to some degree, the culture of their community. Indigenous churches look different from Seattle to Switzerland to Spain. We would expect and rejoice at an African church worshipping to African music, in African dress, with African enthusiasm*

With this understanding, "mission" becomes the very essence of the church as opposed to one function of the church. The church is mission, not a program or an activity in the larger life of the church. As Robert Webber states, "The missional church rejects the association of Christianity with American values and the association of the church with entertainment, marketing, and corporate business models. The missional church is reading both Scripture and culture with new eyes. It sees that what is determined by the Christian faith is more than being a good, upright citizen. It sees the church as something different from the smooth corporate model of business. This emerging church calls for honest, authentic faith that seeks to be church in the way of a more radical discipleship."[17]

Practical Differences Between The Established Church And The Missional Church

Theological difference finds expression in practical ways through ideas, language, and practices. For example, church is characteristically defined in one of several ways.

- *Church as a place: Church is a place you go. The common phrase, "I'm going to church" explains this view. When a person is at the building or facility, they are at church. The implication is that when they are not at the building, they are not at church*
- *Church as an event: Church is something that happens. It is defined by worship services, Bible class, or various other ministries. Again the implication is that when one is not engaged in one of these events or activities, they are no longer doing church*
- *Church as programs or services: Church is determined by what the organization offers: youth programs, special programs and events, fellowship, mission opportunities, etc.*

---

[17]Ancient-Future Evangelism - Robert Webber,

Rather than embodying and demonstrating a new way of living under God's reign, the established church, in general, has been domesticated by American culture. The lifestyles of Christians, their morality, materialism, and a host of other ways of living are fundamentally indistinguishable from its host culture. This translates into an American domesticated corporate entity relying totally on professionalism, marketing, promotion, advertising, and consumerism. With few obvious differences from its host culture, the church struggles to remain relevant to culture as opposed to driving culture.

> "At stake in the confrontation between consumerism and the body of Christ is nothing less than "the continued existence of the church as faithful witness to the mission and character of God, and with it the capacity to think, imagine, desire, and act in ways

> formed by the biblical story."
> —Consumerism, Christian Reflection;
> A Series in Faith and Ethics:
> Baylor University

The task of a missional community is to explore and rediscover God's countercultural call to represent the reign of God in this post-Enlightenment era.

Reconstruction

EVOLUTION OF AN EMERGING

The days immediately after Jesus' death were the darkest, saddest days His disciples ever lived. The whole experience was crushing—almost beyond human endurance. But the unbearable sorrow was turned into inexpressible joy when Mary returned from Jesus' tomb declaring it empty.

During the next five weeks, Jesus appeared, at different times, to all His disciples. On more than one occasion He spent time in *conversation* with His followers. His words were charged with the Kingdom instructions that would shape the coming movement and would soon crest on the men who sat at His feet.

Twelve of them. Count them. Twelve.

Fishermen, taxcollectors—blue-collar workers. These were the men that would lead a movement.

Then it happened.

The sound of wind from heaven entered a room. The room rocked under the fury of its blowing. The Holy Spirit had come and the Kingdom of Heaven had touched earth.

From every corner of the Roman Empire, travelers came and jammed their way into the one square mile that is Jerusalem. Moments earlier the Spirit had come down to clothe man. Now, within the same hour, the Kingdom of God had moved to earth. Three thousand believed the message Peter preached.[18]

Later 5,000 men came to believe[19] along with many priests[20] and thousands of Jews.[21]

A movement was born at a God-ordained time. Not after, not before.

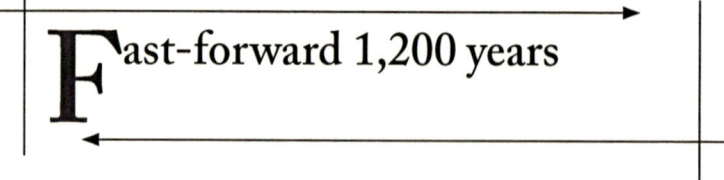

Fast-forward 1,200 years

CONVERSATION ALWAYS PRECEDES MOVEMENT

Believers are most familiar with Martin Luther's 95-point thesis posted on the Castle Church in Wittenberg, Germany

---

[18] Acts 2:38
[19] Acts 4:4
[20] Acts 6:7
[21] Acts 21:20

in 1517. With that posting, Luther challenged the teachings of the Church and sparked a theological debate that led to the Reformation. His dramatic stand left an indelible mark on church history.

In combination with the changes brought on by the Renaissance, Martin Luther set in motion forces that led inexorably to a revolution, which in turn unleashed a massive recalibration in both church theology and praxis.

STANDING AT A CROSSROAD

My background belongs to the Restoration Movement. Its narrative began in the late 17th century and continues today.

The early preachers of the 1800s told stories, debated, and conversed as they traveled the dirt roads between Cane Ridge, Ky., and Nashville, Tenn. to teach the Word of God. The sum of the hundreds (if not thousands) of conversations led to what is known as the Restoration Movement.

Today, restoration churches are approaching the two-century mark in their journey, and they find themselves standing at another crossroads – one that resembles the intersection the movement stood at in the 1850s. In a sense, it's a *deja vu* experience.

The controversy of the 18th century was a clash between

two incompatible theologies.[22] Today, the clash is not one of theology[23] but rather one of praxis.

Unlike the fireside and horseback conversation of the early 1800s, the dialogue of the 21st century is digital. Blogs, online forums, and instant messages are where the conversations gather. The Internet is enabling conversations among human beings that were simply not possible prior to the era of mass media.

There are two spiritual conversations going on today. One inside the attractional, progressive church community and the other online in a new kind-of-church-community.

John Barrett, author of the World Christian Encyclopedia, estimates that there are 112 million churchless Christians - men, women, and children who confess Christ as their Lord but do not belong to any of the traditional churches.

This number is growing fast. Either this is the Great Apostasy or it is a Great Apostolic movement[24] "sent" into the world to walk with it.

Subsequent to Barrett's estimates is a recent study conducted by The Barna Group, a California-based Christian research organization. Their study identified 13 million Americans who called themselves Christian but were "unchurched Christians"... not having attended a Christian church service at any time in the past six months. Revival

---

[22]http://star.walagata.com/w/nucmanchh/Fanning_Richardson.jpg
[23]Among the grace-oriented, progressive churches, theology is generally agreed upon
[24]apostolic means "to be sent"

historian and teacher Andrew Strom called this "a worldwide phenomenon," a calling "out of church Christians."

New Form Of Communication

> Individual blogs are not very interesting in themselves. What is important is how they link to each other to create a massive network.

According to a recent survey, one in three Americans with an Internet connection has read a blog at least once and more than half of blog readers say weblogs influence public opinion (68 percent), mainstream media (56 percent) and public policy (54 percent).[25]

Updated periodically throughout the week, blogs provide online commentary on anything from politics to religion to celebrity gossip. While a small number of blogs have large readerships, countless others have virtually no popularity. The few blogs at the top serve as "gatekeepers" to the rest by linking stories and postings on lesser-known sites. Bloggers and their

---

[25] The findings come from an Ipsos poll conducted from April 14th to April 24th via a representative online US sample of 2,537 American adults.

supporters hail this emerging medium as the innovative arm of the new church. It's where innovation and creativity flourish.

In the past, theological conversations were found in books, magazines, and articles. The emerging conversation is still using books and conferences, but the biggest conversation is linked between blogs. You can't become conversant with the emergent conversation until you go online and start reading the blogs. This is where people go to find out what is being said within the conversation.

With online aggregators, anyone can subscribe to a blog to learn, lurk, or participate. When there is a change in the author or group's weblog, you are notified through your browser. I subscribe to 50 blogs. I know some who subscribe to as many as 250 blogs. This is not a conversation that is taking place in a traditional way. If you think you can go to the bookstore and check out the most recent book and find out what's going on, you'll miss 90 percent of the conversation, which is essentially a grassroots, democratic, electronic, and interpersonal conversation.

Conversational Chaos

As weblogs gain respect and increase in popularity, the emergent conversation gains momentum and deference.

Through non-linear hypertext, new skills are shaped and unstructured federations form. The new leaders are less driven by the clock, are more curious, and conversational. They make extensive use of digital technology that allows them freedom to creatively think, journal, and link their ideas whenever and with whomever they desire.

Through the centuries, the church has adapted to changing social conditions by taking on different forms.

- *The liturgical church was designed to unite a world of oral communities*
- *Denominational churches grew out of the soil of a rational worldview*
- *Less-structured non-denominational churches fit a world of changing novelty*

In spite of the church's proven ability to adapt and survive, none of the forms above will survive for long in the emerging digital culture. But can a movement evolve from a hypertext conversation that appears, at best, in chaos?

An Example From A Culture Of Chaos

China is an orderly, top-down, plan-oriented state with plenty of capitalist drive but not a lot of creativity. The infrastructure in its big cities is first rate. By contrast, India is an unruly democracy—with government as chaotic as its traffic.

With a sense of creative chaos, top Indian entrepreneurs view business problems and opportunities differently than Western leaders—and they come up with strategies that keep the established global business players off balance.

We no longer live in a local, simple world. The effects of globalization are increasingly far reaching and complex and have reached a level where linear tools are virtually ineffective.

Concurrent Converging

In a chaotic, complex, global world, change is frequent and fast, often unnoticed for years - even centuries - as a system is gradually weakened and then, one day, seemingly without notice, the entire system shifts. In nature something shifts 10,000 years ago, and 1,000 years later the Ice Age comes to an end. By geological time—a blink.

The same is true with human culture. A number of concurrent events converge and human culture, societies, and economies seemingly change overnight. The Berlin Wall is an example of this type of shift. Days before its fall, the Soviet system appeared intact and all-powerful. The day after the fall, it was all over and could never be revived.

If futurists could see and correctly interpret events and their subtle shifting patterns and then recognize the converging of these events, humanity could accurately predict an outcome before a cultural shift took place. But since we cannot look into the future, we must wait on change and its resolution.

Order Out Of Chaos

The emerging-missional church has no headquarters and is without formal leadership.[26] From all appearances, there is little order and direction coming through its primary form of communication—hypertext. Yet, paradoxically, in a relational Web,[27] there can be inherent order.

Now, let me return to the thought above: that order can be present in chaos. If you look up at the night sky, you see what appears to be a random collection of stars. But when you take a serious interest in astronomy, you discover that stars are not randomly sprinkled in space but are contained in vast system called galaxies. What was seemingly random has great inherent order. In other words "messy" has order.

A Brief History Of Spiritual Movements

- *The decline of the Church and society in New England of the 1690s was the stage for God's reviving*

---

[26] Brian McLaren is considered its guru
[27] A series of intersecting lines symbolizing a network of relationships

His Church in the 1730s and 40s during what has been called the First Great Awakening. Not only did the Church revive, but the institutions of society were also reformed
- *In the 1790s, slavery and the wealth of industrialization had seduced both the Church and the culture. Again, God revived His Church in the early 1800s and the Second Great Awakening spread across the eastern seaboard*
- *The Third Great Awakening began in 1857 with the Union Prayer Meetings in New York City, against the backdrop of immigrant mass depredations and the failure of the Church to help the poor and needy. In less than three years, cities were changed and it has been estimated that 1 million people came to know Jesus as Savior*

Some have observed that today's emerging conversation is reminiscent of the Jesus people movement in the late 1960s early 1970s. The biggest difference between the two is that the Jesus movement of the 1960s and 1970s was concerned with a post-Vietnam America, a reaction limited to American culture. Conversely, the emergent conversation is a reaction against Christian culture—a global response to the praxis of

Christianity in our world rather than simply a North American-United States-Canadian issue or social response.

STATED GOALS OF THE EMERGENT

Jason Clark[28] is exploring the possibility of an online/print emerging magazine. The goals of the publication are stated as:

- *The bringing together of well-known thinkers involved directly with Emergent and to provide space for the unknowns who have a voice and are directly involved with Emergent*
- *Provide editorial scrutiny from peers before publication, something blogging doesn't at the present (largely) do. In other words, explore the benefits of non blogging media*
- *Help bring more people into conversation with Emergent and each other*
- *Extend the process of communication and resourcing*
- *Bring together the communication that has taken place in books, gatherings, and blogging, into a largely unused media*

Pay attention! We could be watching a number of concurrent events converging.

---

[28] http://www.jasonclark.ws/2006/02/02/emergent_magazi/

Church And Culture

Through the last 250 years, the church has been in decline. No longer does it find itself favorably aligned with its host culture. No longer does Christianity influence culture. Culture now influences the church.[29]

I recently had a conversation with Michael Frost,[30] co-author of *The Shaping of Things to Come*. Listen to one piece of our conversation.

> Mike, how much has the past shaped our current thoughts and models? And how stubborn do you anticipate we will be transitioning from what we are use to, to what is most effective.

Michael Frost: From the moment the Roman emperor Constantine declared the empire to be Christian 1,700 years ago, the church has lived with the self-belief that it is a central pillar of Western society. We have become used to assuming

---

[29] Instead of Christianity driving culture, churches today attempt to become relevant to culture. The attractional church operates out of the belief that it is still in a favored position with its host culture when, in fact, it is not. Church in a missional mode infiltrates culture when in an un-favored position.

[30] http://www.cegm.org.au/staff/frost_michael.htm

that church attendance is a normal and conventional thing to do. We have assumed that our society should listen to us when we make moral pronouncements. In effect, we have believed that we "belong" in the center of the city square and that the other pillars of our society—government, the legal system, the education system, the corporate sector, the artistic community etc. should listen to our perspective and respond accordingly. That no longer works in Western or Eastern Europe. It no longer works in Scandinavia or Great Britain or Australia and New Zealand. And it works less and less in the United States.

We live in a post-Christian age. The church is marginalized and ignored in many parts of the West and increasingly across America. We can no longer assume that a "come-to-us" approach will work. They are no longer coming to us. The breakdown of Christendom has forced us to rediscover ourselves as we were before Constantine: a marginalized, incarnational, missional community of faith. At least this will mean the embracing of a "go-to-them" approach. And yet isn't that what we were intended to be in the first place?

Not many people like change, so of course, there is going to be resistance. But sooner or later, the pain of being a shrinking, ignored community of faith within American culture will be greater than the pain of embracing the change necessary to get out there and engage missionally and generously with the unchurched. [end]

Will the conversation become a movement? I'm not sure. But if it happens, there will be separation, chaos, and reentry—in other words, the letting go of the old and familiar and the embracing of the uncertain new.

Yet I'm not sure a movement will better serve the inevitable than the current conversation does. The conversation alone has and continues to reverberate through Christendom. All one needs to do is go to google.com and count the number of hits with a search of the word emergent.

In my opinion, movements are just easy categories created by historians. If emergent transitions into a movement and takes its place beside the Reformation or the Restoration Movement, it will be heralded by church historians as the first movement to emerge from the digital medium. If it fails, then emergent will be a mere footnote. It doesn't matter what we are called; all that matters is that we move and let future church historians decide whether to label us as a movement or not.

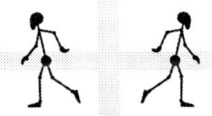

A MISSIONAL MECHANISM FOR THE ATTRACTIONAL CHURCH

As we spin on our cultural axis, Jesus is shining brighter and brighter. History finds us in a post-Christian epoch, but interest in Jesus has never been higher.

For the most part, our society is anti-religious but deeply spiritual. Say, "I'm a Christian" and they flee for their lives. But start a discussion about Jesus, and they gather, they listen, and contribute to the conversation.

Jesus is a bright star in the post-Christian firmament. The quest for the historical Jesus has never been more frenzied. In a roundabout way even the Discovery Channel's "The Lost Tomb of Jesus"[31] is a backhanded compliment to this new era's obsession with Jesus.

What we face can be seen either as a threat or as an opportunity. The people in my circle[32] of influence are more open to spiritual things—including Jesus—than they've been since I've been a Christ-follower. They're hostile toward the church and organized religion but not to Jesus.

---

[31] Written and directed by Simcha Jacobovici; Executive producer James Cameron, writer of Titanic

[32] I'm speaking of the people formerly known as the lost. I have more non-Christian friends than Christian.

The challenge is to present Jesus in containers out of which this culture will clamor to drink.

While Frost and Hirsch directed their groundbreaking book, *The Shaping of Things to Come*, toward the new emerging missional communities and their leaderships, I write for the existing churches hoping and praying that there can still be revitalization for some or at the minimum the planting of missional congregations within broader church structures.

This book will not create space with formulations, only invitation. I have no map that charts a direct route to out-the-church. There are many roads that can lead us there. The best this book can do is encourage you to encounter the Guide who goes with you everywhere.

> The gospels record 132 contacts Jesus had with people. Six were in the temple, four in the synagogues, and 122 were out with the people in the mainstream of life. In this new millennium the call has changed from 'come-to-church' to 'come-to-Christ.'

Relationships

Jesus saved the world by teaching 12 partners how to be family—how to get along and belong to one another. And he still lost one.

When adults were asked to rate five aspects of their lives (relationships, health, personal fulfillment, financial status, and leisure activity), relationship to others and oneself is ranked as the No. 1 ingredient in a quality life.[33] Relationships are the ecology of God's kingdom.[34]

Indian cinema is called "Bollywood" and is known for its formulaic characters. Repetition and familiarity have a special role in Bollywood filmmaking. In fact it is the sense of familiarity that engenders the delight of the moviegoers. Bollywood films are not so much a standalone movie as a flower in a wreath that links people together in the Bollywood universe.

Growing relationships require repetition, especially in our relationships with God, Jesus, and one another. Before we ever step outside our faith borders and walk with the people Jesus misses, it is absolutely essential we unite in the most important thing: loving each other, our Leader, and His cause.

God's greatest hope is that we will join Him in a relationship

---

[33] Research conducted by Taylor Nelson Sofres Intersearch
[34] Humans find it difficult to live with one another even during the best of times. Some of us aren't emotionally wired for intimacy. Some of us have crippling flaws that make relationships difficult. Isaac Newton shunned personal intimacy preferring his laboratory and specimens. Henri Nouwen, who inspired so many to move deeper into relationships with God and one another, had trouble himself developing intimacy with others. Relational disorders abound among creative people.

that turns people who are "accidents waiting to happen" into "people who make things happen."

Someone once said that there are two kinds of people: drains and radiators. We prefer to surround ourselves with the warmth of the heaters than tinker with the underworld of damp, cold, dirty sewer lines. But a big part of the church's ministry is in the drainage business.

How does the American church make the transition from a clean, respectable, middle-class worshiping body of believers to a totally outward-looking, eyes-focused, knees-worn, heart-burdened, missional church?

I have no map with a direct route for outing the church. I have no cut-and-dried formula to transform the thousands of attractional churches into the missional church God is calling us to, but I do have an invitation. Would you allow me another 10 minutes to unpack it?

Perpetual Change

A Christian once told me that *"the church should be the one place on this earth where a person should be able to come knowing exactly what to expect."*

Change often involves loss—feelings of sadness and frustration. It affects us all, but it affects us differently depending where we are in the life cycle. Some people welcome change more when they are younger; some become more comfortable with change when they get older. But change is a fact of life. It is a series of continuous attachments and detachments.

Change in church doesn't always come easily. Thousands of church leaders across America understand the dynamics of change. But not until they interface their understanding of the dynamics with a willingness to challenge the church, in face of potential reprisal, do they become *visionary leaders*.

Unfortunately for the churches that increasingly resist change, there is a place waiting for them on the museum shelf.[35] There will be no Acts 29 movement for the resistant church.

Change is not so much a theological issue (God isn't against change) as it is as a sociological problem (people don't like change). Yet if Biblical purposes are eternal (and they are), it is vital that Christian leaders effectively deal with the sociological problem for the sake of the community's future. Only fluid churches that ride out the rough waters of change will value replacing "once effective" space for the designing of present-future space.

Unpacking this "revolution-invitation" requires the intake of a little background information. I realize church history can be boring, but for us to land on the same page, I ask for your indulgence. So, please stay with me.

---

[35] Some defiantly resist change with the misguided understanding that standing for truth means sisting change.

Sunday School Beginnings

The first Sunday school was designed for the children of chimney sweeps in Sooty Alley, Gloucester. By 1785, the local idea had caught the attention of Christians beyond Sooty Alley, Gloucester and the Sunday School Society was formed. Its stated purpose: to coordinate and develop the Sunday school.

By the 1800s, the purpose of the Sunday school was to provide education and Biblical values for the children of working-class parents. In particular, its purpose was to transmit the values of the "respectable" working class or labor aristocracy. It stressed self-discipline, industry, thrift, improvement, egalitarianism, and communalism. Sunday schools were used not simply to improve literacy and religious knowledge but also to enhance the culture of the working class.

Sunday School: Cultural Position and Purpose

By the middle of the 18th century, Sunday school in America had taken on an evangelistic purpose. Take illiterate people, give them a Bible and a formal education on the one day of the week when they didn't work—Sunday (hence the name Sunday school)—and teach them. At that time, Sunday school was a brilliant evangelistic idea. But, oh, how things have changed!

It's important to mention that throughout the 1700s and 1800s, Christianity was aligned in a favorable position with its host culture. Every Sunday, children, with the blessing of their parents, gathered to learn Biblical values and morals. But over the last 250 years, the church has been in steady decline. Christianity is no longer on Center Street next to Town Hall. She no longer has a strong moral voice. She lives on the margins of her host culture, struggling to remain relevant; a very different position from the early days of the Sunday school.

- *No longer does the church drive culture*
- *No longer does the church have a strong moral voice*
- *No longer is the church at the center of Town Square America*

So I have a few questions—how effective is the 200-year-old Sunday school in this millennium?

Does the original purpose of the Sunday school remain relevant today?

Can it still be considered an evangelistic tool? If not, what is the purpose of the Sunday school/Bible class today? Is it knowledge? (Frost & Hirsch[36] believe learning is more effective

---

[36] The Shaping of Things to Come; Michael Frost and Alan Hirsch

when a faith community is involved in active mission.)

Is the 10 a.m. Sunday school/a.k.a. adult bible class the most effective use of Biblical space today? Or would change better accommodate a Biblical purpose?

Sunday school is wonderful...but only if it effectively fulfills its Biblical purpose in the era it is planted in.[37]

We can count on one thing about the future: how we did things in the past will not be how we do things in the future.

> Just because this is what we've done since the days of Marcus Welby doesn't mean it's still the best way.[38]

Someone has said that it's much easier to birth a new church than it is to resurrect a slumbering one. But I'm not willing to give up just yet.

---

[37] We are in a post-Christian era and the church finds itself in an un-favored position with its host culture.

[38] Dr. Samantha Collier, vice president of medical affairs at HealthGrades, which rates the quality of the nation's hospitals.

Revolution

> The Frontiers of the kingdom of God were never advanced by men and women of caution.
>
> —J. Oswald Sanders

All great missionary movements begin on the fringes of the church. Seldom, if ever, do they emerge from the center. It's vital that in pursuing missional modes of church we get out of the stability of the center and move to the fringes. Engaging the fringes can bring life to the center.[39] Begin by…

- *Encouraging the fringes to follow Jesus*
- *Give away tomatoes from your garden*
- *Help them repair their car or build a porch*
- *Attend their kids' ballgames*
- *Meet them at Starbucks for coffee and talk about Jesus*
- *Attend their mother's funeral and comfort them*
- *Visit them when they are sick*
- *Cry with them, laugh with them*
- *Be transparent; confess your sin; be real*

---

[39] Jesus' ministry was a fringe ministry. Revisit the Gospels and count the number of times Jesus associated with the outcast of His society.

- *Surprise them with kindness*
- *Give a cup of water*
- *No high pressure – let it be natural. If God's moving it, it will go fast (or slow) depending on his will*
- *Love them deeply, forgive their apathy, praise them, win them over with the love of Jesus*
- *Lead by loving – no strings attached*
- *Build friendships, and model the changes. Lead without letting them know it. Show them*
- *Make them want to follow you as you follow Jesus*[40]

Genuinely love the margins! Only after loving the margins will you make inroads to the center. Seek to discern God's specific missional vocation for the entire community and for all its members.

Ignite a groundswell and not far behind will be a grassroots movement.

Now, I need to stop here and say a couple of things before we move forward.

Mission is not limited to the corporate mission. Mission takes place in and through every aspect of life. And this is accomplished through all Christians everywhere. It's what I like to call the sent mandate of the community and the *individual expression of mission.*

---

[40] Thank you, Jim Henderson

I can't overemphasize the importance of training. Ineffective space must be purged for the designing of effective space.

For reasons of clarity, a distinction must be made between necessary organizational structures and institutionalism. Structures are essential for cooperative human actions as well as for maintaining some form of coherent social patterns. But invariably, over time, the increasingly impersonal structures of institutionalism begin to assume roles and authority that ultimately belong to the whole of the faith community in its local and grassroots expressions. This may explain why new births explode and older churches have a tendency to plateau over time.

Create a mess for the cause of Christ. Be subversive. Create excitement at the margins and the end results cannot be ignored.[41]

From Attractional To Missional

Where we need to focus and the direction we must travel to get there is not clear for the vast majority of churches in America.

Remember the worship wars of the 1990s? It took most of that decade for churches to make the transition from traditional to seeker. It may take a decade to make the transition from attraction[42] to missional.

---

[41] I'm grateful for Michael Frost and Alan Hirsch who provide me with many of my thoughts.
[42] Attractional and seeker are synonymous terms

> Every few hundred years in Western society, there occurs a sharp transformation...within a few short decades society rearranges itself—its worldview; its basic values; its social and political structure; its arts; its key institutions...fifty years later, there is a new world and the people born cannot even imagine the world in which their grandparents lived and into which their own parents were born. We are currently living through such a transformation.
> —Peter Drucker: Post-Capitalist Society, New York: Harper's Business. 1993. p. 1.

The trajectory of this transition presents some huge hurdles for the established church. First, the re-direction of the church's emphasis is of utmost importance. The same amount of time must be given to missional crafting as is given to sculpting the Sunday morning worship service. We must talk missional, think missional, emphasize missional, and model missional. Leaders must be missional. Leaders must publicly encourage missional by allocating space and time for the gathered church in the telling of missional stories. Missional must become the centerpiece. Why? Because it was central to Jesus. His ministry was totally incarnational. And we are the second incarnation. We do it for Jesus. It's His calling for us.

But not the least will be the major reallocation of resources. This alone has the potential of forcing the best of us to throw up our arms in frustration and quit. Conversely, I'm very encouraged by the ever-gathering conversation and the coalescence of Emergent Village.[43] Nevertheless, it is an understatement to say it will not be easy.

There is no need to ask for a meeting, disagree with the center (established, institutional leaders), or beg for an evaluation of the effectiveness of the Sunday school/Adult Bible class. There's no need to explain that creating new space would enlighten and enhance the salvation process and remind the faith-community that reaching outward is something they are already doing. Evangelism is not what

---

[43] Around the U.S., friends of Emergent Village meet of their own accord, at their own time and place, and discuss what they choose. What binds the cohorts together is a common desire to be in robust and respectful conversation about things that matter.

we thought or what we were taught for the better part of our Christian life.[44]

But without a grass roots movement clamoring at the feet of leadership, missional will never gain a foothold. Without a swelling at the margins, leaders will forever fight to maintain the status quo.

REFLECTIONS ON MISSIONAL TRAINING

Training should emphasize the development and momentum to resist the centripetal attraction of exclusive, self-obsessed Christian fellowship. Sustaining a centrifugal ministry requires a commitment to mission—a holistic way of being Christian, a culture, a lifestyle that is comfortable functioning without the regular weekly church structure, that is able to draw on a diffuse set of spiritual resources, that is innovative and creative in generating community and in providing mutual support. At the very heart of it all must be an instinctive enthusiasm for developing "cross-border" spirituality. This will require both patience and time. Training is teaching first and maintaining second.

Whereas in recent years spirituality has been driven by Bible study, we would need to see a shift in the direction of a less confident, exploratory mode of relating to God where we

---

[44] Most of us are already doing what Jesus would want us to be doing. But there are some very important elements missing and need to be regularly emphasized. Hence, the need for ongoing training.

explore our way out of the narrow confines of traditional evangelicalism into a missional space where theological reflection becomes more meaningful.

There is no particular template for cross-border communities. They could be small or large, short-term or long-term, personal or impersonal, organized or disorganized. Cross-border communities will depend on the development of an outlook, a way of life, and a sense of personal empowerment for the apprentice of Jesus in this complex, paradoxical, yet fascinating landscape we call the post-Christian world.

Perhaps one key criterion is the need to get ourselves to a point where in relating to pre-Christians we can say that we are on common ground. We must find that point where our journeys converge so that we can build relationships on the basis of spiritual commonality.

THE TRAINING PIECE

How training advances is something each community must determine on the basis of location and need. This Missional Training Model would replace the Sunday school/Bible class and would include, but not be limited to, the following:

Apprentices will live with and among a particular people group or a setting where they will learn principles and gain

practical experiences in actually ministering (and failing) – and/but continually learning from the results. Emphasis on learning will include "praxis" as well as theoretical models. Settings would include: the downtown district, cultural minority, suburban contexts, and professional contexts.
- *Mission teams would form around shared emphases, such as: local community concerns, challenges, obstacles, affinities, interests, problems, projects, or work schedules*
- *Mission teams, targeting specific groups move among people, listening to learn, providing hands-on (loving, intentional, incarnational) ministry, resources, and encouragement. They would engage every aspect of that culture to bring salt and light into those contexts.*

On the first Missional Sunday, everyone in the community would be introduced by occupation. Over the next few Sundays, each person is identified and recognized for his or her service outside the church.

The whole church is introduced to:
- *The public official in the congregation who is tackling important quality of life and social issues in the community*
- *The medical practitioner who has changed his approach*

to patients by providing counseling and practical support rather than just curative care
- *The schoolteacher who has just started work in an inner-city school with many students from broken homes.*

There are no big Christians, and there are no little Christians. There are no distinctions between laity and professional for we are all Christ-followers incarnating the world Jesus incarnated. We are the second incarnation.

Every Sunday morning before worship we hear from the community.

We hold hands up.

We clap.

We create space—missional space.

Jim Henderson's *Doable Evangelism*[45] is adapted to the community and becomes the standard for equipping and teaching the concept of Ordinary Attempts (Evangelism for the Rest of Us).[46] Missional Training is not on a six- week track. Missional Training is forever.

---

[45] < http://www.doableevangelism.com/>
[46] < http://www.off-the-map.org/oa/oa_guide_intro.html>

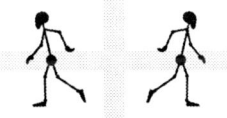

THINK GLOBALLY ACT NEIGHBORLY

How times have changed! Look around you. Notice anything different?

Okay, I'll help us get started. For the next few paragraphs, let's consider something we're all familiar with—the retail store, better known as the modern department store. What used to be the staple of the American shopping landscape has nearly diminished to the point of no-return. Yes, there are a few department stores still around but those that have survived have had to re-invent themselves by dismissing the order, formality, and stillness of the old stores.

SHOPPING ENTERTAINMENT

Modern retailers are just coming to grips with the consequences of the breakdown of hierarchy and the fragmentation of narratives.

Uniforms are out, as are standard décor, shelving, and presentation. There is no hierarchy of goods - watches compete with perfume, luggage with high fashion, cafés with fast food. We listen to reggae while we watch a Western, eat at McDonald's for lunch and local cuisine for dinner, wear Paris perfume in Tokyo and retro clothes in Hong Kong and knowledge—well knowledge is a matter for TV games.

Like the American shop owner of the 21st century, the faith communities that thrive will embrace fragmentation by catering to one niche.

Bath and Body Works caters to those with a penchant for fragrance and bath. *Linen and Things* to bed, bath, and the best of linens. *American Apparel*[47] sells pricey T-shirts to consumers who care just as much that those who sell them are well-treated and happy employees; *American Apparel's* niche is moral as well as economic.

This chapter is what I like to refer to as "designed space." So keep that in mind as we use the above example from commerce and the indigenous behavior of the American consumer in our metaphorical application to the Christian community.

One niche—with intention—for the sake of Christ!

As we rally around one niche, we're going to have to plow through a few paragraphs on theology. It's essential! Are you ready? Let's go.

---

[47] <http://www.americanapparel.net/>

Process And Event

The process of salvation is as important as the event. For as long as I can remember, faith communities have emphasized event over process. Yet God is just as interested in the turning points (process) on the continuum of life as he is in the consummation of the process in the event (baptism/sinner's prayer). I have a friend who didn't become a Christ-follower until after the death of his mother. Her death was a turning point in the process that led to his conversion (event).

I had a conversation with a skeptic that was published in New Wineskins Magazine.[48] When we talked, he asked me not to reveal his identity.

"…just refer to me as SuperSkeptic."

Our conversation is part of SuperSkeptic's journey. It's also part of mine. If you read it, it will become part of your journey as well. I may never cross SuperSkeptic's path again. Yet I felt no urgency in convincing him that my convictions are something he needs to adopt. SuperSkeptic is in the middle of a process, and I refuse to contravene its course.

Decades of involvement in "church" programs and full-bodied Christian fellowship pulled me away from the people Jesus seeks until a paradigm shift in the early 2000s moved me away from the comforts of my former life as a Christ-follower

---

[48] <http://www.wineskins.org/>

to a life with a more missional bend. Now, for the first time, I find myself with more non-Christian friends than Christian and more road stories than church stories.

Creating "safe places" for the people Jesus' misses is something I'm very passionate about.
- *No timetables*
- *No agendas*

Call me a fellow explorer seeking to foster genuine friendships with the people Jesus' misses the most. If it so happens that a person's spiritual development matures while in relationship, I pray I'll be the one given permission to become their spiritual guide. But before this will happen, I must find that point where our journeys converge and then allow time for the building of a relationship on the basis of a spiritual commonality.

Process Evangelism

Modernism played tricks on us. In one way it tricked us into confusing the expression (worship teams, do we sing with instrumental accompaniment or not, acoustic, drums, and on and on) with the purpose (missional).[49] If you asked a Christ-follower in the late 1980s or early 1990s if they were

---

[49] I base my conclusion on priorities I see in churches – worship preparation far exceeds missional preparation.

interested in attending an evangelism class they would quickly remind you that they, *"...were just not gifted to do evangelism."* If anyone were going to make an evangelistic attempt (as defined by the modern era) it would be the local paid preacher. But when salvation is viewed as a process everything changes.

First, and foremost, it takes away the "I'm not gifted" slogan. Whether we realize it or not, we all make evangelistic attempts. Modernism mislead us. Evangelism is not some thing left to the gifted evangelist. Evangelism is an ordinary attempt. (Jim Henderson of *Off the Map* birthed this idea.)[50] It may sound trite and simple, but let me emphasize how indispensable ordinary attempts are. Ordinary attempts endow evangelism with a very important interlude in the evangelistic process by creating potential turning points in the lives of the people Jesus' misses. Ordinary? You bet it's ordinary! But at the same time—very, very intentional.

INTENTIONAL BUT ORDINARY?

I always have my automobile's oil changed at the same station. Over time, I've come to know the attendants. They call me Mr. Peatross until I tell them, "...Call me Fred." Now we're on a first name basis. As our relationship evolves I find them talking to me about their marriages, their stressful

---

[50] See Jim Henderson's Web site at <http://www.off-the-map.org/ >

encounters during the day, and more.

Whether it's an oil change or groceries or a trip to the UPS Store, I make more than a purchase; I make a trip that is intentional (it's my niche). And when I leave a store I begin praying behind my friend's back.

OUT THE CHURCH

Last week, as my office was being moved to another location, a fellow employee stopped by to visit me. I can't remember exactly what was said, but in the context of our discussion he called me a "different kind of Christian." He said, "You're not the run-of-the-mill, stereotypical Christian."

When he left my office I knew without a doubt that he had just given me the greatest compliment a Christian could ever hope for. Later, he informed me that, because of expansion, his office space was being taken. He asked if I would want to share my new office with him. As coworkers, friends, and fellow-explorers we walk this journey together.

If the church is going to turn the corner on the consumerist twist it finds itself caught up in, it will do so because leaders involve themselves in building a culture of the ordinary evangelist (a faith-community niche).

Jesus' apprentice is not going to be formed through Sunday

morning sermonettes, drama, worship teams, or edifices fit for comfort but through clear, intentional teaching that says evangelism is forged through a process of salvation. And ordinary attempts are the turning points. Now, here's something you might not know. Every Christian makes ordinary attempts.

But Christians need to be made aware:
- *They need to understand that the process of ordinary is as important as the event of salvation*
- *They need to understand how significant and important their role is in the process of salvation*
- *Christ wants them to know!*
The vision must come alive!
Teach it! Practice it! Talk about it every time the community gathers!

It's time we rally around a niche and there is none more important!

Make your Sundays a time for ordinary stories among ordinary Christians! Culture building…until Christ comes back! So…

Do we invite the missing to our environment? Or follow Jesus' mandate to "GO" and walk with them in their environment?

In 1988, I traveled to India to tell the story of Jesus. After a night of village preaching, my translator and I traveled back to Hyderabad (my home base in India). As we drove through the night, my translator became overly excited about a thought he had. When I asked about his excitement he said—*"Someday we will come to your country as missionaries."*

At the time his statement seemed very strange. I didn't think much about it; I simply sloughed it off as a dream or window into America and a symptom of his desire to be like Americans (it seemed all Indian preachers made rather sloppy attempt to dress like us). Now, almost 20 years later, his statement appears prophetic.

In *Lost in America*, authors Tom Clegg and Warren Bird point out that *"...the unchurched population in the United States is so extensive that, if it were a nation, it would be the fifth most populated nation in the world."*

Imagine! Our unchurched population the largest mission field in the English-speaking world and the fifth-largest globally! Something tells me my Indian friend was right. But how is this possible when nearly every street corner in America has a church building sitting on it?

If we got out more, we might know more. Road stories are crucial. Like the early Christians, we need to, once again, become known as people *of the way. How?*

- *By walking with and listening more to what the people*

Jesus misses the most have to say
- *Drop the infamous slogan "We hate their sin but love the sinner," and actually get to know and become a fellow sinner's best friend*

What this means is more time away from church buildings and church functions and a change in our ministry paradigm. Are we ready for that?

The idea of taking church ministries off our campuses is not a new or novel thought.[51] Remember Joshua? He sent out a couple of secret agents to spy out the land of Jericho.

If we really desire to reach out to this culture, we're going to have to become like the spies Joshua sent out and boldly walk across our faith borders[52] and engage the land God wants to give us.

It's time we break out of our Christian circles, stop the busyness of church, face outward, take a look, and experience the world beyond the borders of our community gatherings.

Yes, it will require training[53] and patience and time for a

---

[51] Are we ready to connect with culture by taking our ministries out of the church building and placing them in different buildings all over the city? Most churches would never do this, for lack of a vision narrative. Yet, mobile ministries that move beyond the confines of a "one-building" or "one-campus church" are first concerned with the ones Jesus misses most and show this by attempting to minister to people throughout the city they find themselves in.

[52] When I say 'borders' I mean edifices, campuses, and the like. Anyplace that could or has become a comfortable faith zone.

[53] The origin of the Sunday morning bible class comes out of evangelistic efforts to teach Biblical principle under the cover of an English class. Since this is no longer the goal of the Sunday morning Bible class I suggest we drop the Bible class for training classes.

vision narrative to mature a culture of Christians who intentionally make ordinary attempts.

Uniting Around A Vision

Philosopher John Ruskin contends that "…the greatest thing a human soul ever does in the world is to see something, and tell what he saw in a plain way."

The Lord said close to the same…

One day Philip found Nathanael sitting under a fig tree (John 1:43-51). Philip told Nathanael, "We have found the one Moses wrote about in the Law, and about whom the prophets also wrote—Jesus of Nazareth, the son of Joseph."

"Nazareth! Can anything good come from there?" Nathanael asked.

"Come and see," said Philip.

This is what visionaries do—help people see. Remember the metaphor I used at the beginning of this little booklet?

"…embrace fragmentation by catering to one niche."

ONE VISION

Culture building—through intentional missional training. All for the sake of Jesus!

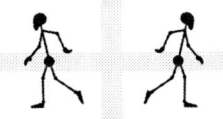

THE IMPORTANCE OF PERCEPTION

The church-centric environment arose from the modern era and is the context in which Christians adopted their belief of and praxis on evangelism. The inappropriateness of Friends Days, Fireman Sundays, and all those other "Will you come to church with me?" exercises rank alongside the picketing of abortion clinics, the loud and unswerving *"Christian"* position on embryonic stem-cell research, the outspoken moral correctives, and the negative vitriol of the religious right. We've had the cart before the horse, and it's time to turn it around.

What images come to the mind of the non-Christian when they watch Christians picket abortion clinics[54] on the evening news? What images appear when they hear Christians condemn all who would support embryonic stem cell research or when believers rail against homosexuality? Are unbelievers perceptions strengthened when Christians erect inconsiderate and unthoughtful billboards on major interstates for the eyes

---

[54] Traditional tactics used by anti-abortion activists include protests, picket lines, and even attempts to intimidate abortion-clinic workers at their homes. Recently, though, a new tactic has arisen: buying the property used by abortion clinics and then refusing to renew their leases. This gets rid of the clinic for good, whether they want to go or not.

of all to see as they drive by? It's not about right or wrong—at least not initially. It's about perception.

> Don't call yourself a *Christian* and vote for a candidate that supports *abortion* and *homosexuality!*
>
> "Do you love me? Then keep my commandments"
>
> ~Jesus Christ

Public Billboard on a major highway

> There are things known and there are things unknown, and in between are the doors of perception.
>
> —Aldous Huxley

So are the perceptions any different when the non-Christian hears a standalone church invitation offered by a Christian?

> "We are having a Friends Day at our church and I would like it if you would consider coming with me."
>
> "It takes seven invitations to get one person to come."

I paint with a broad brush here but even so, I feel it is a fair assumption to say that we fail in our perceptions when we blindly make our pitch without an understanding of the echoes deep within the hearts of our friends, co-workers, and neighbors. And not until we get to know them, listen to them, and develop sensitivity to their perceptions of what constitutes "normal living" will we earn the right to invite them to experience, on our turf, the things important to us.

Here's what I have learned.

- *Live within the boundaries of what they have defined as normal*
- *Genuinely like them*
- *Refuse to call them lost* [55]
- *Count your conversations not your conversions*
- *Spend more time with the non-Christian than the Christian*
- *In group socialization avoid outnumbering the non-Christian*
- *In the early stage of a relationship avoid praying in front of them—God hears closet prayers*
- *Make time for vacationing with non-Christians*

In 2003, Paula and I vacationed in Costa Rica. In 2006 we vacationed in Italy. On both vacations we traveled with

---

[55] Lost carries the sound of finality. When the thousands of loved ones lost family members in the Twin Towers on 9/11 they refused to call them lost. They called them missing.

non-Christians friends. And on both occasions, we had a wonderful time. When we traveled to Costa Rica our party included three young women from Colorado whose vocabulary was frequently sprinkled with colorful metaphors; two middle-aged couples from Atlanta whose worldviews were very different from ours; and a South African couple who had moved to Costa Rica to become caretakers of the El Castillo, our point of destination.

For two weeks, we lived together at the El Castillo, a castle in the rain forest overlooking the Pacific Ocean. We laughed together, played together, told our stories, but most important we showed mutual acceptance of one another.

Drinking was part of this group's day, but we never raised an eyebrow; we even joined them for an occasional beer. When my wife and I read the Bible in the morning, I could sense a little uneasiness in the beginning, but soon they became familiar with our routine and accepted our daily Bible intake. As a sign of trust, they began sharing small parts of their lives. It was obvious that we had convinced them that we were normal people—just like them. Suddenly, we were missionaries who had stepped across familiar borders to engage our friends on their ground. Each day, our relationships grew. We had become spiritual explorers walking alongside our new friends.

Three days into our trip, my wife asked the group if it would be okay to have a morning devotional. The questions flowed. The group granted us permission to help them connect the dots in their life story. We had created a safe place on their dominion where life was lived by their code of conduct. Each night I prayed behind my non-Christian friends' backs and then told them to their face over a morning bagel.

> The church has spent enormous amounts of time and energy planning programs for teaching the unchurched. We've redesigned church parking lots, reprinted our brochures, repainted our Sunday school rooms, and even gotten flashy web sites up and running, but the battle isn't happening in our buildings. It's in our backyards.
> —Jim Henderson; a.k.a Lost, p.31 ; Water Brook Press

DETERMINED

The realization that the majority of those who read this book will be the pioneers of future church is exciting to me. Yet as a part of me responds with a smile another part recoils in fear. Something deep within welcomes the challenge, knowing that it is through challenging times as these that spiritual strength is increased. As the hymn writer said, we are not "carried to the skies on flow'ry beds of ease."[56] The journey from the attractional mode of the Western church to the missional is a rugged transition, full of trials that along the way could hurt us.

But I'm committed to stay until the end - to have the determination of Nehemiah and stay strong and focused on the confidence of God's sovereign control regardless of the Sanballats and Tobiahs and Geshems who cross our paths. I've abolished the word "quit" from my vocabulary.

Frontiers require pioneers who refuse to quit, acquiesce, or compromise. But God will honor in you what he honored

---

[56] Isaac Watts, "Am I a Soldier of the Cross?

in Nehemiah—determination.

Here are four suggestions for frontier living:
- *Never be surprised by the surprises of transitions*
- *Keep a positive perspective. Rehearse your objectives and remember that God is in full control. Like Nehemiah, focus with determination. Allow nothing to dissuade you from the pursuit…no criticism, no clever scheme, nothing. For that to happen you must…*
- *Fight your battles on your knees. Nehemiah's journal is punctuated with prayers. He prayed for help. He prayed for wisdom. He prayed for strength, and so should we.*
- *Stay close to others*

God never meant for us to do this alone. We stay in touch through our writings and blogs. None of us is totally self-sufficient. When you look at the lifestyles of the settlers of the last century, you discover that they quickly learned the value of staying close. With any acquisition they quickly built sod huts in the middle of their acreage but found that they were vulnerable and exposed. When help was needed, it was too far away, which usually spelled disaster. They learned to build their homes at the corner of their property, not too far from their neighbors who built on the corner as well. A "cluster" of homes built in fairly close proximity made a lot more sense when threats arose from attacks or sickness invaded or fire broke out. Life was strengthened when blessings and hardships were experienced together. As the old Swedish proverb states, "Shared joy is double joy; shared sorrow is half sorrow."[57]

> I pray the words in this book have encouraged and renewed your determination.

---

[57] Bruce Larson, There's a Lot More to Health Than Not Being Sick (Waco, Texas: Word Books, 1981), p.

EPILOGUE

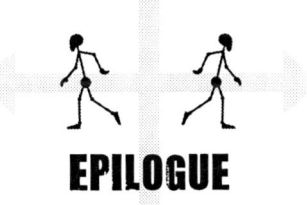

I pushed the button and took the parking ticket from the meter. Turning the corner I pulled in to what appeared to be the only parking space on the lower level of the parking garage. I put the car in park, placed the metered ticket on the dashboard and walked through the garage. Feeling my friend might be waiting on me, I hurriedly crossed the street dodging in between two cars stalled in traffic to the other side. I picked up my pace as I rounded the corner. Breathing passably deeper I walked into Starbucks and quickly glanced around the room. Realizing my friend had not arrived yet I walked outside and grabbed one of the iron chairs on Starbuck's patio and waited.

"How long have you been waiting?"

"Not long, only a few minutes," I said.

"Hey, I'm hungry do you mind if we walk across the street to the Marshall Café?"[58]

As I drank a glass of tea and my friend ate a salad we caught

---

[58] The Marshall University Hall of Fame Cafe is a 300 seat restaurant dedicated to Marshall University athletics

up on our families, the good, confessed the bad, and thought about what might be next.

I wish you knew my friend. You would leave with a clear impression, a Jesus impression. My friend leaks Jesus out of every pore in his body.

Characterizing Missional

"It wasn't until I moved to Huntington that I heard the word missional. I don't get how it is any different than it has always been. We treat our friends and neighbors as we would want to be treated, we engage people; encourage everyone, like I just did for that waitress. I encouraged her with my words and a mega tip. That's missional isn't it?"

How could I argue with that? My friend is correct. It's how we treat people; this is salvation's process.

"But just imagine if every Christian did as you just did," I said.

"Imagine if Christians were cognizant of every person's place in salvation's process. Envision what could be, if through culture building every Christian became intentional for Jesus. Don't you think we should, at the least, give as much time and attention to building a culture of missional Christians as we do in preparing for Sunday worship? After all worship is a by-product of the Christian life not a primary stance we display before the world."

My friend seemed to agree but stated a problem worth thinking about.

"I love people. I'm a people person. I'm constantly with people. I want to be. I can't say it enough. I love people. But people are the problem. The best I can do is live the missional life before others and then pray it makes a difference. Maybe you already leave good tips after someone serves you well but I left that mega tip for both you and the waitress."

It was at this point that my friend's wisdom shined through.

"Fred, I don't think you realize how much of the Christian leader's time is consumed in helping a faith community. There's sin, there's divorce, there's hurt, there's family dysfunction, selfishness, and a host of other problems that robs people and keeps them from finding the energy and time necessary to become intentionally missional. And, on top of all that, I must balance my remaining time with the thing I love as much as the people I serve—studying God's Word. That's something I need. That's something I love to do. And those same people that have so many problems, the people I love, the people I sometimes cry with—they want to hear from the Lord and they need to hear from the Lord. And you can be sure that I'm going to make sure that they do."

"Freddy, I do the best I can to model missional, but..."

REFLECTIONS ON THE WORD BUT

For the remainder of the day I've thought about what my friend said.

I'm a writer. I live by theory. I live between the paragraphs and chapters. It's easy for someone like me to believe that the words I write are perfectly fitted to cure the problem. But...

My friend is a practitioner. He's bright. He's genuine. He's honest. He cares about people. He loves Jesus and he loves the faith community he leads. He lives missionally. He knows people. But...

Maybe Frost and Hirsch were correct when they said...

> *Right up front we want to confess our belief that the planting of new, culturally diverse, missional communities is the best way forward for the church that views itself in a missional context. The challenging context in which we live in the West requires that we adopt a fully missional stance. While some established churches can be revitalized, success seems to be rare from our experience and perspective. We believe that the strategic focus must now shift from revitalization to mission, i.e.*

from a focus on the "insiders" to the "outsiders"; and in so doing we believe the church will rediscover its true nature and fulfill its purpose.

…the real hope lies with the courageous leaders who will foster the development of alternative, experimental, new communities of faith.[59]

But maybe my good friend provided a caveat we haven't given full consideration.

Whether we call it the conventional church or the missional church the problem of humanity; sin and selfishness—has the potential of curbing any faith community's intentionality and missional effectiveness beyond what I might believe. But…

I will remain a pioneer who refuses to quit, acquiesce, or compromise.

---

[59] The Shaping of Things to Come; Frost & Hirsch: pg. x

APPENDIX

A phrase my friend used on the footer of a church bulletin was used as a platform for launching this book, "creating environments that connects us with Jesus and people." (see the book's Introduction).

Now listen to my friend's thoughts on creating the kind of environments that connect us to Jesus and people.

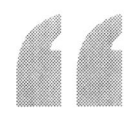

"

We've learned so much about God's creativity by studying the Old Testament, especially the book of Exodus and Leviticus. God's instructions for how to construct a tabernacle is amazingly detailed. It is so comprehensive and detailed that, at times, it has left me scratching my head in wonder.

Why is this so important to God?

Why did he choose the colors (e.g., gold, blue, purple, scarlet)?

Why did he choose the fabric? Why did he choose the particular wood and metal?

Why did he give the craftsmen special gifts to make it just like he wanted?

Why did he prescribe the incense?

Why did he give detailed instruction for so many different offerings and animal sacrifices?

Why all the attention to diet and holidays? Why?

Because God was creating an environment for people to connect with him and each other. Worship was central yet generalized to every aspect of life. Worship engaged all the senses; seeing, hearing, touching, and even tasting the fellowship offerings. And the beauty of the model does not compare with the glory of what John describes in Revelation - our eternal home.

When Jesus saw how the religious leaders had ruined God's temple he drove them out with a whip. Twice! They had ruined the environment by turning it into a den of thieves. He accurately predicted its destruction and pointed us to heaven. Jesus said he was going to prepare a place for us but before Jesus takes us to this perfect environment - our home in heaven - he made His home in our body.

Jesus lives in you and me. The Holy Spirit leads us to others as the Father calls them. I've seen him work in AA meetings, restaurants, city streets, homes, hospitals, and jails. A few years ago I served time in jail. But this is where God set me free. Ironic? Not *really. God shows up everywhere if you look for him. He's made his home in me and he wants me to create safe environments everywhere I go. I do it with a smile. I engage people, smile at them, brag on them, praise them, and when the Holy Spirit opens their heart I put in a good word for Jesus. It is just that simple. No matter where you go or where you are Jesus is with you. He wants to connect, not only with you; he especially wants to make his home in the hearts of those who do not know him. So create warm safe environments in small groups, homes, coffee shops, schools, AA meetings, hospitals, jails - wherever you go love people and keep it simple, easy to understand. Go about doing good things for people and put Jesus Christ in the center and watch the Holy Spirit work. He will connect you with Jesus and people.*

Connecting

Loving

Healing

Encouraging

That's what Jesus wants us to do. Don't ruin the environment with a bad attitude or a critical spirit.

Target pain

Pay attention to the hurt in people and meet their felt needs

Divorce

Depression

Anxiety

Addiction
Guilt
Grief

Find where they hurt and show them you care. Create the environment by being completely humble, patient, loving, and empathic – then – once they know you care and understand – ask Jesus to make the connection.

This is it! This is how we create environments that connect us with Jesus and people!

Shalom

"Fred's friend is Jeff Garret."

Printed in the United States
84989LV00002B/55-63/A